F·R·I·E·N·-D·S
The Television Series

Lessons on Life, Love, and Friendship

By Shoshana Cohen Stopek

RUNNING PRESS

PHILADELPHIA

Hachette Book Group supports the right to free expression and the value of copyright. The purpose of copyright is to encourage writers and artists to produce the creative works that enrich our culture.

The scanning, uploading, and distribution of this book without permission is a theft of the author's intellectual property. If you would like permission to use material from the book (other than for review purposes), please contact permissions@hbgusa.com. Thank you for your support of the author's rights.

Running Press
Hachette Book Group
1290 Avenue of the Americas, New York, NY 10104
www.runningpress.com
@Running_Press

Printed in China

First Edition: October 2012

Published by Running Press, an imprint of Perseus Books, LLC, a subsidiary of Hachette Book Group, Inc.

The Hachette Speakers Bureau provides a wide range of authors for speaking events. To find out more, go to www.hachettespeakersbureau.com or call (866) 376-6591.

The publisher is not responsible for websites (or their content) that are not owned by the publisher.

Library of Congress Control Number: 2012943031

ISBN: 978-0-7624-4614-8 (hardcover)

TLF

21   20   19   18   17

"How you doin?"

From 1994 to 2004, Thursday nights were the best of the week—the night I would religiously join the ranks of 25 million other Americans to hang out for half an hour with our beloved friends. Created by Kevin Bright, David Crane, and Marta Kauffman, the Emmy-Award winning show featured six friends navigating life and love in Manhattan as they approached (or avoided) their thirties.

As more and more Americans began identifying with the adorable quirks of Ross, Rachel, Chandler, Monica, Joey, and Phoebe, the series quickly became a pop culture phenomenon and one of the most popular sitcoms of all time. More importantly, though, the characters warmed our hearts with their laughter, tears, romances, heartbreaks, and comic escapades to become a part of our everyday lives.

I attended a live taping of *Friends* during its ninth season. The

experience was exactly what you'd expect—amazing. The actors displayed natural camaraderie and ease with one another. When they messed up a line, they laughed about it, and it made them even more likeable. At the end of the taping, some of the actors hugged each other—just like real friends, which is exactly what they had become. The characters/actors had become so interchangeable and familiar to me I was almost compelled to run up on stage and join in the hugs . . . but I contained myself.

It is this chemistry among the cast and the connection we developed with them that touched many of our lives for the better. At the end of the day, what we all long for is love and companionship. And maybe sometimes it's the fictional kind that makes us work that much harder on the real. What we all want in a friend, after all, is to know that they're there for us. And just as *Friends* has shown us, it's our duty to be there unconditionally for them. So pop in that famous theme song, grab a latté and your best friend, and relive some of the invaluable lessons on life, love, and friendship that *Friends* has taught us.

Growing up ain't easy . . . so have a back-up plan.

Monica: You can't live off your parents your whole life.

Rachel: I know that! That's why I was getting married.

Preserve guy code.

Joey (re: Ross): Can you believe he's only had sex with one woman?

Chandler: I think that's great. You know, it's sweet.

Joey: Really?

Chandler: Are you kidding? The guy's a freak.

Monica: Let go! I'm a tiny little woman! . . . 42 to 31. Like the turkey, Ross is done!

Girl talk is necessary.

Rachel: I can't believe he hasn't kissed you yet. God, by my sixth date with Paolo, he'd already named both my breasts.

You may get "hung up" on a friend.

Ross: Let's hang up on three . . . one, two, three, well you didn't hang up either!

[Rachel hangs up on Julie for Ross.]

Maintaining the advantage.

Ross: You're over me? When were you . . . under me?

Work out
with friends
of the
opposite sex.

Monica: Come on, give me five more. Five more . . . five more and I'll flash you.

Women's intuition is a powerful force.

Phoebe: I knew something had to be wrong. My fingernails didn't grow at all yesterday.

Sometimes you have to create "space" in a relationship.

Ross: Now, just as she's about to drift off, you hug her, then you roll her over to her side of the bed—she still thinks you're just hugging—and you slip away. Hug for her. Roll for you.

Beware of power tools.

Joey: Oh, sorry. Did I get ya?

Chandler: No, you didn't *get* me! It's an electric drill! You get me, you *kill* me!

Never mess with a
man's underwear.

Joey: You hide my clothes, I'm wearing everything you own.

Chandler: Oh my God! That is so *not* the opposite of taking somebody's underwear!

Joey: Look at me—I'm Chandler! Could I *be* wearing any more clothes? Maybe if I wasn't going commando!

Keep a really big stick
on hand just in case
you need to check your
neighbor's vitals.

Joey: Ugly Naked Guy looks awfully still.

Phoebe: Oh my God! I killed him! I killed another one! And this curse is getting stronger, too, to bring down something that big.

Team work and winning are not always synonymous.

Ross: You go long.

Rachel: How long?

Ross: 'Til we start to look very small.

Make a nautical statement in your living room.

Joey: You think I have $1,200? I'm home in the middle of the day, and I got patio furniture in my living room. I guess there's a few things you don't get from book learnin'.

How to "excite" friends into moving furniture.

Ross: I drew a sketch about how we're gonna do it. Okay, Rach, that's you; that's the couch.

Rachel: Whoa, what's that?

Ross: Oh, that's me.

Rachel: Wow! You certainly think a lot of yourself.

Ross: No! That's ... that's my arm.

Chandler: I thought you really, really liked your new couch.

Girlfriends
+ wedding dresses
+ beer
= the perfect date

Rachel: I gotta tell ya, this really does put me in a better mood.

As Best Man, remind the groom that you're running the show.

Joey: Listen, I know it's your party, but I'd really like to limit the number of museum geeks that are gonna be there.

Ross: Tell ya what. Let's not invite any of the anthropologists; just the dinosaur dudes!

Joey: Okay, we'll need a six-pack of Zima.

Beware of creepy coffee house guys, unless they're giving you free lattes.

Gunther (to Rachel re: kissing Phoebe): We kissed . . . and I've been feeling guilty. . . . So, are we cool?

Rachel: Okay.

Gunther: I knew you'd understand.

A little self-affirmation never hurts.

Phoebe: Hi, I'm Phoebe Buffay and I have babies coming out of me.

Promote good self-esteem in your children at an early age.

Phoebe: It seems like only yesterday I was talking to you in a little petrie dish.

Old photos will help
you feel like you've really
matured. Unless,
of course, you haven't.

Chandler: I can't believe how stupid we used to look.

When in doubt, play it cool.

Ross: So Rach, does it feel different since I've been away at college?

Rachel: Not really.

Ross: That's cool.

Joey: It's stuck. Plus it smells really bad in here.

Joey: Maybe we can lure them [the baby duck and baby chick] out. Do you know any birdcalls?

Chandler: Oh tons. I'm quite the woodsman.

It's hard to be modest when you know you're the best.

Ross: Hey, when the snippy guy sees "The Routine," he'll wanna build us our *own* platform!

Monica: Was it really that good?

Ross: We got honorable mention in the Brother-Sister Dance category!

Always share happy news among friends.

Ross: We're having a girl! (Everyone hugs, then looks at Chandler.)

Chandler: I'll catch ya later.

How to create your own unique holiday spirit.

Ross (as the Holiday Armadillo): Merry Christmas. Oh, and Happy Hanukkah!

Monica: Be-cause armidillos *also* wandered in the desert?

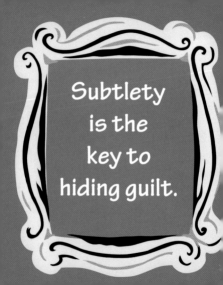

Joey: No one needs to know where we were.

Ross: You may want to lose the foam finger.

No wish is too big on your 30th birthday.

Rachel: Can I keep the presents and still be 29?

Napping with
friends promotes
bonding . . . and
sometimes paranoia.

Ross: What happened?!

Joey: I don't know!

Ross: We fell asleep, that is all.

Joey: I'll talk to you later.

Ross: But not about this . . . no touch, no touch.

Learning
to ride
a bike can
be scary.
Good
friends
will help you
through it.

Ross: You have to learn how to ride a bike.

Phoebe: Why do I have to learn?

Ross: In case of emergency. What if a man comes along and puts a gun to your head and says you have to ride this bike or I'll shoot you.

Phoebe: I would ring the bell . . . and then knock the gun out of his hand with a Chinese throwing star.

Don't try to change your partner into something he's not.

Monica: It was either a pink bunny or no bunny at all.

Chandler: No bunny at all. Always no bunny at all.

Sometimes your friends
really need a pep talk.

Ross: You gotta let me win.

Chandler: My wife thinks I'm a wimp.

Ross: At least you have a wife. I keep getting divorces and knocking people up. And I'm dressed as doodie.

Chandler: You're Sputnick.

Ross: Who we kidding? I'm doodie.

Keep it short and sweet.

Joey: I've known Monica and Chandler for a long time, and I cannot imagine two people more perfect for each other. And now, as I've left my notes in my dressing room, we shall proceed to the vows.

Why registries were invented.

Monica: Are you sure you peed on the stick right?

Rachel: How many ways are there to do that?

Monica (re: taking the test again): You gotta take it now. Do it as a present to me.

Don't mock good literature.

Rachel: You've learned some new moves!

Ross: This guy at work gave me a self-help book as a joke. Who's laughing now?

Why women really have babies.

Monica: We have twins! Now I have twice as many lives to control!

~~~~~~~~~

Safety first.

Ross: There's no seat belt.

Phoebe: That's ok, if we hit anything the engine will explode so, you know, it's better if you're thrown from the car.

Play up your strengths.

Ross: What we have is too important to mess up over some girl. We can get laid anytime we want.

Chandler: I had sex in high school.

Ross: Me too. I'm good at it.

Always dress appropriately.

Phoebe: I got married! Could someone get me a coat? I'm freakin' freezing.

Don't enrage the chef
or she'll lock you
out of the kitchen and
chop off your head.

Joey: We want you to know
that we're very, very sorry.

Chandler: The floating
heads do make a good point.

When your hair
takes the day off...

Chandler: I think this is the first time in our marriage that I felt like the more attractive one.

Monica: I've had it with the hair jokes. Tomorrow morning, before we leave, I'm going to the salon.

Chandler: Okay, Buckwheat.

Root for your friends.

Phoebe: Rachel and Joey! It's Rachel and Joey!

Monica: Oh my god, I love how thin these walls are.

Always maintain a healthy curiosity.

Rachel: Aren't you just a little curious what it would be like?

Joey: Am I curious? I'm as curious as . . . George.

Sometimes a little sugar-coating works.

Rachel: You know that feeling when you're trying to blow a Saint Bernard out your ass?

Love really is blind.

Chandler:
You look so great.
I love you.

Don't fight nature.

Joey (re: Chandler turning 30):
Not Chandler. We're all getting
so old. Why are you doing this
to us? Why, God, why?

Sexy talk in the kitchen is underrated.

Monica: I love carrots. Sometimes I like to put them down here like this while I talk to you.

Encourage your friend's new endeavors.

Chandler:
I think it's the dying cat parade.

Why sleepovers are fun.

Rachel: Rachel Green is very happy you're in her room . . . I just don't want to be alone tonight.

Ross: I could maybe grab a sleeping bag.

Your friends always have your back.

Ross: Should I climb down your front so we're face to face or down your back so we're butt to face?

Joey: How much do you weigh?

Ross: I prefer not to answer that right now. I'm still carrying a little holiday weight.

Confidence is key to hooking up.

Rachel: College guys are so cute.

Monica: You have a boyfriend.

Rachel: I know, but if some guy wants to kiss me tonight I am so gonna let him.

When you really like someone:

Chandler: So how you doin'?

Rachel: Bitchin'.

Chandler: Hi Monica.

Monica: Hi Chandler. Really nice to see you. . . . Not!

Stall doors were invented for a reason.

Ross: Uh, Joey, some people don't like that.

Joey: Ooh, someone's flossing.

Put on your smile and best party hat when a hooker shows up to your fake bachelor party.

Joey: Why would she go in the bedroom?

Chandler: So she's a . . .

Joey: Yup, that's one naked hooker.

Male bonding is good for the T-zone.

Monica: Hey girls.

Ross: In ten minutes we're gonna have younger looking skin.

It's not the clothes that make the man.

Monica: Find some [clothes] please. Anything that doesn't say I died tragically in France.

Keep your friends close.

Phoebe: Ah, Catwoman, so we meet again.

Monica: So we do, Supergirl.

Phoebe: It's me, Phoebe!

Remember your friends have your best interests at heart.

Phoebe: Joey's asleep. After he passed out, we put the sand around him to keep him warm.

This book has been bound
using handcraft methods and
Smyth-sewn to ensure durability.

Designed by Corinda Cook.

Written by
Shoshana Cohen Stopek.

Edited by Cindy De La Hoz.

The text was set in Avenir,
Flama, Rockwell, and Tekton.

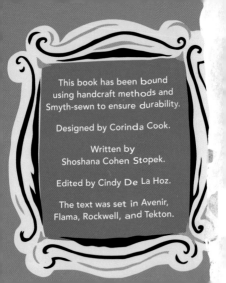

This book has been bound
using handcraft methods and
Smyth-sewn to ensure durability.

Designed by Corinda Cook.

Written by
Shoshana Cohen Stopek.

Edited by Cindy De La Hoz.

The text was set in Avenir,
Flama, Rockwell, and Tekton.